Peyo

PUSSYCAT

PAPERCUT Z ™

NEW YORK

Peyo GRAPHIC NOVELS AVAILABLE FROM PAPERCUTZ™

THE SMURFS

1. THE PURPLE SMURFS
2. THE SMURFS AND THE MAGIC FLUTE
3. THE SMURF KING
4. THE SMURFETTE
5. THE SMURFS AND THE EGG
6. THE SMURFS AND THE HOWLIBIRD
7. THE ASTROSMURF
8. THE SMURF APPRENTICE
9. GARGAMEL AND THE SMURFS
10. THE RETURN OF THE SMURFETTE
11. THE SMURF OLYMPICS
12. SMURF VS. SMURF
13. SMURF SOUP
14. THE BABY SMURF
15. THE SMURFLINGS
16. THE AEROSMURF
17. THE STRANGE AWAKENING OF LAZY SMURF
18. THE FINANCE SMURF
19. THE JEWEL SMURFER
20. DOCTOR SMURF
21. THE WILD SMURF

- THE SMURFS CHRISTMAS
- FOREVER SMURFETTE
- SMURF MONSTERS

PUSSYCAT

BENNY BREAKIRON

1. THE RED TAXIS
2. MADAME ADOLPHINE
3. THE TWELVE TRIALS OF BENNY BREAKIRON
4. UNCLE PLACID

THE SMURFS ANTHOLOGY

— VOLUME ONE
— VOLUME TWO
— VOLUME THREE

THE SMURFS AND FRIENDS

— VOLUME ONE

THE SMURFS #1-20, THE SMURFS CHRISTMAS, FOREVER SMURFETTE, and SMURF MONSTERS graphic novels are available in paperback for $5.99 each and in hardcover for $10.99 each; THE SMURFS #21 graphic novel is available in paperback for $7.99 each and in hardcover for $12.99 each; BENNY BREAKIRON graphic novels are available in hardcover only for $11.99 each; and THE SMURFS ANTHOLOGY, THE SMURFS AND FRIENDS, and PUSSYCAT are available in hardcover only for $19.99 each at booksellers everywhere. Order online at papercutz.com. Or call 1-800-886-1223, Monday through Friday, 9 – 5 EST. MC, Visa, and AmEx accepted. To order by mail, please add $4.00 for postage and handling for first book ordered, $1.00 for each additional book and make check payable to NBM Publishing. Send to: Papercutz, 160 Broadway, Suite 700, East Wing, New York, NY 10038.

THE SMURFS, BENNY BREAKIRON, and PUSSYCAT graphic novels are also available digitally wherever e-books are sold.

PAPERCUTZ.COM

PUSSYCAT

© *Peyo* - 2016 - Licensed through Lafig Belgium - www.smurf.com

English Translation Copyright © 2016 by Papercutz. All rights reserved.

Joe Johnson, SMURFLATIONS
Adam Grano, SMURFIC DESIGN
Janice Chiang, LETTERING SMURFETTE
Matt. Murray, SMURF CONSULTANT
Martin Satryb, GROUCHY SMURF
Brittanie Black, SMURF COORDINATION
Michael Petranek, ASSOCIATE SMURF
Suzannah Rountree, ASSOCIATE SMURF
Bethany Bryan, ASSOCIATE SMURF
Jeff Whitman, ASSISTANT MANAGING SMURF
Jim Salicrup, SMURF-IN-CHIEF

ISBN: 978-1-62991-150-2

PRINTED IN CHINA
THROUGH FOUR COLOUR PRINT GROUP
OCTOBER 2016 BY SHENZHEN CAIMEI PRINTING CO., LTD.

Papercutz books may be purchased for business or promotional use. For information on bulk purchases please contact Macmillan Corporate and Premium Sales Department at (800) 221-7945 x5442.

DISTRIBUTED BY MACMILLAN
FIRST PAPERCUTZ PRINTING

PEYO AND THE PUSSYCAT(S): AN ADVENTURE IN TIME AND SPACE

BY MATT. MURRAY, SMURFOLOGIST

Felicitations, feline fanatics! Welcome to this very special Papercutz anthology designed to showcase Peyo's kitty comic PUSSYCAT.

As many of you ailurophiles — that means "cat lovers" — may or may not know, Peyo was the man behind the creation of everyone's favorite little blue gnomes from Belgium, the Smurfs (whose adventures are also available from Papercutz as single graphic novels and in THE SMURFS ANTHOLOGY collected editions), and the cartoonist whose name is still signed by the art studio which continues his work in comics decades after his passing.

When one is asked to think of a feline character that has sprung from Peyo's pen, surely the cat that will probably pitter patter across that person's mental landscape would be Azrael, the mangy orange and white fleabag that has terrorized the Smurfs in comics and on television and movie screens the world over. Azrael made his first appearance in the 1959 mini-comic *Le voleur des Schtroumpfs*" (the expanded and translated edition of which can be found in THE SMURFS #9 "Gargamel and the Smurfs" as well as THE SMURFS ANTHOLOGY Vol. 1) and has returned numerous times often serving as a logical, cynical, and ironic foil to and commentator on the bumbling antics of his owner, Gargamel. In the decades since his first appearance, Azrael's smart aleck charms have helped cement his role as one of the most memorable villains in THE SMURFS canon and earned him a stint as

one of the chief characters on THE SMURFS animated series— which had its initial run on American television from 1981 to 1990 and continues in reruns worldwide dozens of years later.

The long-lasting global popularity of that program insured the fact that when THE SMURFS made the jump to the "big screen" (in the two SMURFS live-action/CGI hybrid films released by Sony Pictures Animation during the early 2010s), Azrael and his human cohort Gargamel would go along for the ride giving them new life as flesh and blood (and in Azrael's case sometimes pixilated) char-

Pierre Culliford AKA Peyo

acters that were not only inspired by, but almost identical to their ink and paint counterparts.

For nearly six decades Azrael has been *the* cat in Peyo's cartoon continuum and entertainment empire, but what if I were to tell you that he had an older brother? Not a litter-mate that maliciously meowed across the medieval countryside with the likes of Gargamel or chased Papa and Brainy through the forest and into the Smurfs Village, but another cartoon kitty that both pre-dates the creation of Peyo's most popular characters by a decade, and exists in a world centuries after those adventures.

If I were to ask even the most hardcore of Blue Believers — that's what we call our SMURFS supporters — how many would know about PUSSYCAT?

Odds are, if the fans in question are from English speaking countries and born after say, 1992, the likelihood of them having seen or even knowing about PUSSYCAT (or as he's known in his native French, *POUSSY*) is pretty slim — as his exploits have never been translated and exported outside of Europe until now.

So, it becomes my pleasure to introduce this comprehensive collection of PUSSYCAT comics collected and translated into English for the very first time almost seven decades since his first appearance. But, before we get down to the lovely illustrations and some of the laughs that Peyo (and later artists who worked for him in his Belgian studio) would put on the page; let's take another leap back through time.

If you were an illustrator or cartoonist working in the mid-20th Century, the work you aspired to— due largely to the exposure and, if your work developed a regular following, the job security— was that of a newspaper comic creator. In a large number of print newspapers worldwide, comic strips were given their own page, then their own section, sometimes even their own supplements which could be removed from the paper and enjoyed on its own by young and old alike. They were not necessarily viewed as "kid's stuff" and early characters such as the Yellow Kid, Buster Brown, and— wait for it— Krazy Kat, were actually more the providence of adult fans than young readers, and much like the wider "graphic novel" market of the early 21st Century there was a wide selection of styles and subjects which were not just limited to adventure strips or romance comics, kids' comedies or— wait for it— funny animals.

Now, if you picked up the two clues I dropped rather clumsily in the previous paragraph, you'll begin to see where this rambling trip is taking us… and with that I welcome you to the aforementioned pit stop over post World

War II Brussels. Strap your goggles on, and let's take a look at a young man named Pierre Culliford who'd recently lost his job as an assistant animator when the company he worked for *La Compagnie belge d'actualités* (CBA), shut its doors in light of a cultural embargo being lifted and a flood of American animated cartoons, like the *Looney Tunes*, flooding and dominating the theatrical market.

Pierre, a teenager who had previously dropped out of trade school and took the animation job out of financial desperation, found that he enjoyed being an artist but had difficulty finding regular work because of his age and overall lack of experience. While his friends and former colleagues, most older and more seasoned than he, were able to find jobs illustrating for newspapers and magazines (with some even landing prized slots in comics journals— magazines which published long form serialized comics stories, where artists could develop their own characters and stories that could then be collected into their own large format books called "albums" and sold separately), Pierre found himself painting lampshades and shopping bags for local businesses.

Understanding that cartooning was a business as much it was an art form, Pierre was determined to make it despite his perceived limitations and in the next few years set about creating a number of characters and series that he understood to be popular and commercial hits for publishers. His "stable" included *Capitain Coky*— a pirate strip, *Inspector Pik*— an adventure comic inspired by the popular *Tintin*, *Tenderfoot*— an action comedy starring a Native American brave and his scout, *Johan*— medieval adventure comic inspired by Errol Flynn's films, and— wait for it— *Poussy*, a funny animal cartoon built around single panel gags. He signed the comics using a nickname his English-speaking cousin gave him years before: Peyo.

Peyo shopped those concepts around to a lesser level of success, having some strips, namely *Johan*, appear sporadically in newspapers such as *Le Dernière Heure* (The Latest Hour) and after doing a few magazine covers and some spot illustrations for other local publications, he was able to sell his first *Poussy* comic, as a single panel gag which appeared in the January 22, 1949 edition of *Le Soir*. Although his *Poussy* strips were infrequent, they were popular, which lead to the publisher to purchase additional material from Peyo and migrate *Johan* over to that paper paving the way for the success that comic would eventually become. (*Johan*, which was sold in 1946 to *Le Dernière Heure*, gained some traction in *Le Soir* and after an introduction to the publisher *le journal Spirou*, one of the major comics journals of the day, *Johan* would land there and eventually grow into a recurring strip and a minor cultural phenomenon that would, in 1958, feature the debut of *les Schtroupfs* or as English-speaking countries know them: the Smurfs.)

Now, let's try to tie it all back together and take a look at the environment in which *Poussy* was first sold, mainly from the perspective of animation, a field Peyo was familiar with at the time. And not just from his prior work in the industry, but in his previous fulltime work as a film projectionist, where, it should be noted, he fell in love with the work of Walt Disney Productions.

The 1940s fall right in the middle and are often considered the height of what's known as the "Golden Age of American Animation." The aforementioned *Looney Tunes* series was in full swing for Warner Bros. studio, and rival companies such as MGM were directly producing now classic short films, while other competitors such as Paramount and Fox contracted regular work from animation studios such as Fleischer Studios and Terrytoons, respectively. Then, there was Disney who produced not only exquisitely artistic full-length feature films, but different series of shorts which would run before them. Arguably, the most popular style of cartoon was — you don't even have to wait for it this time — the funny animal, because as the Egyptians had taught us all thousands of years ago, people are amused by seeing other creatures take on human traits and, as they have in stories throughout time, mirror our own faults back at us.

While most known animal species were anthropomorphized in one studio's set of cartoons or another to varying degrees of success and popularity, and some became more iconic than others — a certain mouse and one company's bunny rabbit come to mind, each studio did have one consistent staple in their stables — this time I'll wait for you to say it…

You're right! A cat!

MGM had Tom (originally Jasper) who was locked in eternal combat with Jerry the Mouse; Warner had Sylvester who was trapped in a similar relationship with Tweety Bird; Terrytoons morphed one of the human villains, Oil Can Harry, into a cat for the express purpose of taking on their popular funny animal hero Mighty Mouse; and then there was Disney, who offered a slightly more kind and

gentle interpretation of a cartoon kitty when they plucked Figaro from their 1940 feature film Pinocchio, to star in short cartoons as Mickey Mouse's housecat.

One should note that of those characters, Peyo's Poussy bears the closest resemblance to Disney's Figaro, as both are more genteel and closer in reality to the everyday nature and exploits of common housecats, as opposed to the sensationalized, rather violent, and somewhat existential worlds of Tom and Sylvester. To our regular Smurfologists, or those who have read my introduction to Peyo's SMURFS AND THE MAGIC FLUTE in SMURFS ANTHOLOGY VOL. 1, that idea should come as no surprise as I mentioned that during his life Peyo went on record as saying that Disney's work was a source of both direct and indirect inspiration throughout his career.

So, time-travelers there are some of the "why"s and "wherefore"s of the PUSSYCAT strip (and even some tidbits about THE SMURFS) but I'd be remiss if I didn't get into some of the "when"s and "how"s about the publishing history of what you're about to enjoy.

For that we can pick-up the thread of our time trip in the early 1950s, when Belgian newspapers began to focus their attention on youth readership and created supplements with articles intended for young readers and a larger selection of comic strips to entertain them. *Le Soir's* offering was *Soir jeunesse* (Evening Youth) which from 1955 to 1960 ran POUSSY in an expanded four-panel format.

Unfortunately due to the popularity of *Johan* — now called *Johan and Pirloit* (Peewit in English) in the pages of *Spirou* and of course the rise of the Smurfs, Peyo, ever the businessman, had to abandon *Poussy* and focus on those more lucrative properties. Over the next few years though, the money and attention that *Johan* and *The Smurfs* brought in allowed Peyo to revisit old concepts and expand his enterprises and hire additional writers and artists to help develop and execute his ideas for those properties as well as some dormant ones such as Pussycat.

In an issue dated November 4th, 1965, *Poussy* made its first appearance in the pages of *Spirou*. At first, the comics magazine just re-printed colorized gags that originally appeared in *Soir jeunesse*, but by February 1969 they had exhausted that supply, and Peyo and his publisher found that the public still had a hunger for pussycat cartoons.

To meet the demand, Peyo drafted one of his former assistants on THE SMURFS, Lucien De Gieter, to work with him on new *Poussy* strips. Although no formal record of who exactly contributed what to the process, or how much actual drawing Peyo might have done himself, we do know that De Gieter drew at least 47 gags signing all but one of those, and it's quite possible there are more that he didn't sign. After that run of comics, there was another three year hiatus, and when Poussy returned Peyo was working with another assistant, Daniel Desorgher, who produced 16 gags.

In 1989, some 12 years after those cartoons ran in *Spirou*, Peyo and his company had created their own comics magazine, *Schtroumpf* (if you remember, the original Franco-Belgian word for Smurf) and they commissioned a new series of 21 gags created between 1989 and 1992, by the likes of Daniel Desorgher, Eric Closter, and Philippe Delzenne.

As previously mentioned, this is the first time almost all of these *Poussy*— here known as PUSSYCAT comics are being published for an English speaking audience, and probably the first time that market has seen or even heard of the character (although he is mentioned and had a couple of images appear in my 2011 book *The World of Smurfs…*, which chronicles the history of Peyo and his creations up to the theatrical release of the first live-action/CGI Smurfs film.)

French and Belgian collections of the strips have been published dating back to the 1970s (*Spirou's* publisher, Dupuis released albums of re-printed *Poussy* comics after its run in their magazine), but it should be noted that

some, and not all of the original strips, made it into those hardcover collections. Moreover, Peyo and Dupuis chose to present those thematically and not in order of publication. It's only been recently that an effort was undertaken to re-print all of the Pussycat comics chronologically, and it is those efforts that this volume is based on and inspired by.

We at Papercutz have tried to maintain as consistent a format as possible to facilitate your comics enjoying experience, but you will notice over the course of this particular publication that the comic's art and presentation evolve and change as the strip jumped from publisher to publisher over the years.

You may also notice a numbering system which at some points seems inconsistent, especially in relation to the *Spirou* gags — not surprising as *Spirou* had both French and Belgian editions, and sometimes comics would appear in one that didn't appear in the other, and in some cases comics published in both failed to make it into the albums published years later. (EDITOR'S NOTE:

Despite our best efforts, we failed to locate gag #253. Either Peyo "skipped" a number, and this gag doesn't exist, or, as some think, it's the editorial content "The dignified turkey," which appeared in the *Journal de Spirou* #1706 of December 24, 1970— thus, after gag #252 and before gag #254— and which serves as #253. Or this gag does exist. And we'd be very happy to add it in lieu of this text in any new printings of this complete collection. If you have any information on this subject, please don't hesitate to bring it to our attention.)

But, whatever you do, please do not let this little conundrum stand in your way of enjoying what we have put together, which is the most comprehensive, exhaustively researched, and enjoyable collection of Pussycat the English-speaking world has ever experienced… and with that, I'll stop taking up your attention and turn you lose to spend the rest of your time enjoying the adventures of Pussycat. ●

PUSSYCAT

This very first "Pussycat" gag, *Poussy, le chat* appeared in *Le Soir* #21 of January 22, 1949.

PUSSYCAT AND THE FISH

Poussy et le poisson appeared in *Le Soir* #42 of February 12, 1949.

PUSSYCAT AND PAPA LUSTUCRU

Pussycat et le Père Lustucru appeared in *Le Soir* #63 of March 5, 1949.

PUSSYCAT AND HIS SON

Pussycat et son petit appeared in *Le Soir* #77 of March 19, 1949.

PUSSYCAT HAS A NICE DREAM

Pussycat fait un beau rêve appeared in *Le Soir* #105 of April 16, 1949.

PUSSYCAT AND THE DOGS

Pussycat et les chiens appeared in *Le Soir* #133 of May 14, 1949.

PUSSYCAT AND THE FUR

Poussy et la fourrure appeared in *Le Soir* #147 of May 28, 1949.

PUSSYCAT HAS AMBITIONS

Poussy a de l'ambition appeared in *Le Soir* #175 of June 25, 1949.

PUSSYCAT AND THE NEST

Poussy et le nid appeared in *Le Soir* #196 of July 16, 1949.

PUSSYCAT DOESN'T LIKE BATHS

Poussy n'aime pas le bain appeared in *Le Soir* #217 of August 6, 1949.

PUSSYCAT AND THE ALARM CLOCK

Poussy et le reveille-matin appeared in *Le Soir* #238 of August 27, 1949.

PUSSYCAT AND THE FLYPAPER

Poussy et le papier collant appeared in *Le Soir* #245 of September 3, 1949.

PUSSYCAT AND THE LOBSTER

PUSSYCAT AND THE SEVEN-LEAGUE BOOTS

Poussy et le homard appeared in *Le Soir* #280 of October 8, 1949.

Poussy et les bottes de sept lieues appeared in *Le Soir* #301 of October 29, 1949.

PUSSYCAT AND THE VACUUM CLEANER

PUSSYCAT IS VERY STYLISH

Poussy et l'aspirateur appeared in *Le Soir* #322 of November 19, 1949.

Poussy est très coquet appeared in *Le Soir* #343 of December 12, 1949.

PUSSYCAT AND THE MECHANICAL MOUSE

Poussy et la souris mécanique appeared in *Le Soir* #350 of December 17, 1949.

PUSSYCAT AND THE MAGNIFYING GLASS

Poussy et la loupe appeared in *Le Soir* #364 of December 31, 1949.

PUSSYCAT PLAYS WITH A BALLOON...

Poussy et la souris mécanique appeared in *Le Soir* #350 of December 17, 1949.

PUSSYCAT MEETS A MOUSE

Quand Poussy rencontre une souris appeared in *Le Soir* #49 of February 18, 1950.

PUSSYCAT PLAYS HOT ROD…

Poussy joue au bolide… appeared in *Le Soir* #62 of March 4, 1950.

PUSSYCAT AND THE GOLDFISH

Poussy et le poisson rouge appeared in *Le Soir* #132 of May 13, 1950.

PUSSYCAT IS TOO HOT

Poussy a trop chaud appeared in *Le Soir* #209 of July 29, 1950.

PUSSYCAT GETS REVENGE

Poussy se venge appeared in *Le Soir* #19 of January 20, 1951.

PUSSYCAT AND THE KITE   PUSSYCAT AND THE FISHERMAN

Poussy et le cerf-volant appeared in *Le Soir* #117 of April 28, 1951.   *Poussy et le pêcheur* appeared in *Le Soir* #131 of May 12, 1951.

At the beginning of the Fifties, Belgian daily newspapers expanded their columns for the young. They became veritable weeklies, in one or two large, front-and-back pages that were foldable and formed mini-magazines of 8 or 16 pages. That's how the new *Soir Jeunesse* (Evening Youth) came into being. After that, comic strips came to occupy a more important space. After a long break, Pussycat continued his antics in the *Soir Jeunesse* from September 1955 to 1960. From then on, these gags would occupy a more comfortable space. Always comprised of four rectangular panels, they always offered a flexibility of presentation, even if the configuration was different, since each gag could be presented either in two levels horizontally or, the next time, standing on end vertically. To facilitate legibility, we have placed all of the following strips on two levels.

After a second long break, it's only in 1965, in issue #1438 of November 4th, that Peyo's cat comes to the pages of *Journal de Spirou*, (*Spirou* magazine). Initially, the gags which had appeared in *Soir Jeunesse* and were set to color were the ones to be republished, through February 13, 1969. But they appear in *Spirou* out of order. In this unabridged collection, we have put them back in the chronological order of their creation.

Some of them were later republished in hardcover comic albums, others not. That's why the presentation of the following gags is different. For those which appeared in albums, it seemed a better idea to keep the book's page layout in order to preserve the vignette and the gag's title. All the same, some of them have neither a title nor a vignette: they're the first gags of the chapters. Peyo had, in fact, grouped his gags thematically (and not at all chronologically). For each chapter, there was a small introductory text and a drawing. You'll find them all at the end of this collection.

For those that didn't appear in comic albums, we've kept the original "*Spirou* banner." It should be noted that all the gags that appeared in *Spirou* weren't necessarily in both Belgian and French versions. A certain number appeared only in the French version.

 PUSSYCAT BY Peyo BOOBY-TRAP

Gag #1 appeared in *Spirou* #1495 of December 8, 1966.
It was later republished in album 1, page 7, in January 1976.

PUSSYCAT BY Peyo

Gag #2 appeared in *Spirou* #1573 of June 6, 1968.
It was later republished in album 1, page 25, in January 1976.

PUSSYCAT BY Peyo   TIT FOR TAT

Gag #3 appeared in *Spirou* #1546 of November 30, 1967.
It was later republished in album 3, page 11, in October 1977.

PUSSYCAT

Gag #4 appeared in *Spirou* #1547 of December 7, 1967.
It was later republished in album 1, page 9, in January 1976.

PUSSYCAT BY Peyo

Gag #5 appeared in *Spirou* #1550 of December 28, 1967.
It was later republished in album 3, page 24, in October 1977.

Gag #6 appeared in Spirou #1569 of May 9, 1968.
It was later republished in album 3, page 32, in October 1977.

A BIG BITE

Gag #7 appeared in *Spirou* #1551 of January 4, 1968.
It was later republished in album 1, page 42, in January 1976.

PUSSYCAT BY Peyo

Gag #8 appeared in *Spirou* #1553 of January 18, 1968.
It was later republished in album 3, page 37, in October 1977.

PUSSYCAT THE HAIR-DRESSER APPRENTICE

Gag #9 appeared in *Spirou* #1635 of August 14, 1969.
It was later republished in album 3, page 39, in October 1977.

PUSSYCAT BY Peyo   VANITY UN-FAIR

Gag #10 appeared in color in *Spirou* #1561 of March 14, 1968 in France and in black and white in *Spirou* #1566 of April 18, 1968 in Belgium.
It was later republished in album 3, page 39, in October 1977.

PUSSYCAT A MOUTHWATERING SMELL

Gag #11 appeared in *Spirou* #1552 of January 11, 1968.
It was later republished in album 2, page 10, in January 1977.

PUSSYCAT BY Peyo

GUARD CAT

Gag #12 appeared in *Spirou* #1563 of March 28, 1968.
It was later republished in album 3, page 20, in October 1977.

PUSSYCAT BY Peyo

MASKED BALL

Gag #13 appeared in *Spirou* #1503 of February 2, 1967.
It was later republished in album 2, page 31, in January 1977.

PUSSYCAT BY Peyo — THE SLEEPWALKER

Gag #14 appeared in *Spirou* #1498 of December 29, 1966.
It was later republished in album 3, page 18, in October 1977.

PUSSYCAT — A SKILLFUL PREPARATION

Gag #15 appeared in *Spirou* #1499 of January 5, 1967.
It was later republished in album 1, page 41, in January 1976.

PUSSYCAT BY *Peyo*

Gag #16 appeared in *Spirou* #1654 of December 25, 1969.
It was later republished in album 2, page 44, in January 1977.

PUSSYCAT AN INCRIMINATING PUDDLE

Gag #17 appeared in *Spirou* #1554 of January 25, 1968 and was used again in *Spirou* #2009 (October 14, 1976), #2012 (November 4, 1976), and #2013 (November 11, 1976).
It was later republished in album 1, page 35, in January 1976.

Gag #18 (subsequently renumbered 117 for unknown reasons) appeared in *Spirou* #1601 of December 19, 1968.
It was later republished in album 3, page 44, in October 1977.

PUSSYCAT BY Peyo

Gag #19 appeared in black and white in *Spirou* #1570 of May 16, 2015 in France and in #1585 of August 29, 1968 in Belgium.
It was later republished in color in album 2, page 3, in January 1977

PUSSYCAT BY Peyo — THE BABY'S BOTTLE

Gag #20 appeared in *Spirou* #1567 of April 25, 1968.
It was later republished in album 1, page 11, in January 1976.

PUSSYCAT BY Peyo — MIGHT IS RIGHT

Gag #21 appeared in *Spirou* #1578 of July 11, 1968.
It was later republished in album 1, page 17, in January 1976.

 **PUSSYCAT** BY Peyo PETTY THEFT

Gag #22 appeared in *Spirou* #1574 of June 13, 1968.
It was later republished in album 1, page 40, of January 1976.

PUSSYCAT A PEACEFUL COEXISTENCE

Gag #23 appeared in *Spirou* #1500 of January 12, 1967.
It was later republished in album 1, page 17, in January 1976.

PUSSYCAT — THE OLD RECORD PLAYER

Gag #24 appeared in *Spirou* #1514 of April 20, 1967.
It was later republished in album 2, page 28, in January 1977.

PUSSYCAT — THE PHOTOGRAPHER AT THE CASTLE

Gag #25 appeared in album 2, page 38, in January 1977.

PUSSYCAT BY Peyo

Gag #26 appeared in *Spirou* #1555 of February 1, 1968.
It was not published in album format.

PUSSYCAT BY Peyo

Gag #27 appeared in *Spirou* #1580 of July 25, 1968.
It was later republished in album 2, page 26, in January 1977.

PUSSYCAT BY Peyo

A BAD SHELTER

Gag #28 appeared in *Spirou* #1571 of May 23, 1968.
It was later republished in album 1, page 18, in January 1976.

PUSSYCAT DEMONSTRATION OF AFFECTION

Gag #29 appeared in *Spirou* #1512 of April 6, 1967.
It was later republished in album 1, page 6, in January 1976.

PUSSYCAT BY Peyo

APRIL FIRST

*Translator's note: The expression in French for "April Fools" is "Poisson d'avril" or "April Fish."
Gag #30 appeared in *Spirou* #1510 of March 23, 1967.
It was later republished in album 2, page 7, in January 1977.

PUSSYCAT BY Peyo

A GOOD DEFENDER

Gag #31 appeared in *Spirou* #1494 of December 1, 1966.
It was later republished in album 3, page 9, in October 1977.

PUSSYCAT BY Peyo

Gag #32 appeared in *Spirou* #1631 of July 17, 1969.
It was not published in album format.

PUSSYCAT BY Peyo — SONG FOR SONG

♪ AH! I LAUGH TO SEE MY FIGURE SO LOVELY IN THIS MIRROR....! MARGUERITE... ♪ *

Heavens! Eleven o'clock already! It's high time I went to bed!... Goodnight, little Pussycat!

MEOOOWWw

*Translator's note: This is a famous "Jewel Song" aria from **Faust,** and also performed by Bianca Castafiore in **Tintin.**
Gag #33 appeared in *Spirou* #1586 of September 5, 1968.
It was later republished in album 2, page 28, in January 1977

PUSSYCAT BY Peyo

Gag #34 appeared in *Spirou* #1583 of August 15, 1968.
It was later republished in album 2, page 34, in January 1977.

PUSSYCAT BY Peyo   SERENADE

Gag #35 appeared in *Spirou* #1509 of March 16, 1967.
It was later republished in album 1, page 41, in January 1976.

Gag #36 appeared in *Spirou* #1582 of August 8, 1968.
It was later republished in album 2, page 16, in January 1977.

PUSSYCAT BY Peyo

THE BURGLAR AGAIN

Gag #37 appeared in *Spirou* #1589 of September 26, 1968.
It was later republished in album 3, page 21, in October 1977.

PUSSYCAT BY Peyo   CAT'S CONSCIENCE

Gag #38 appeared in *Spirou* #1508 of March 9, 1967.
It was later republished in album 3, page 30, in October 1977.

PUSSYCAT BY Peyo   SELFISH ADMIRER

Gag #39 appeared in *Spirou* #1564 of April 4, 1968.
It was later republished in album 3, page 9, in October 1977.

Gag #40 appeared in *Spirou* #1590 of October 3, 1968.
It was later republished in album 3, page 8, in October 1977.

 PUSSYCAT BY *Peyo* DOORBELLS

Gag #41 appeared in *Spirou* # 1506 of February 23, 1967.
It was later republished in book 1, page 7, in January 1976.

PUSSYCAT THE SAUSAGE THAT GOES BOOM

Gag #42 appeared in *Spirou* #1587 of September 12, 1968.
It was later republished in album 1, page 37, in January 1976.

PUSSYCAT BY Peyo   A TUSSLE

PUSSYCAT!

MEOOOW

WOOF WOOF WOOF

HSSSS

Rover! Here!

You can't keep your dog on a leash?

What about you? For starters, your cat's the one who provoked Rover!

Liar! It was your filthy mutt who started it!

Filthy mutt? I dare you to say that again!

Gag #43 appeared in *Spirou* #1595 of November 7, 1968.
It was later republished in album 1, page 18, in January 1976.

Gag #44 appeared in *Spirou* #1596 of November 14, 1968.
It was later republished in album 3, page 30, in October 1977.

PUSSYCAT BY Peyo

Gag #45 appeared in *Spirou* #1501 of January 19, 1967.
It was later republished in album 1, page 28, in January 1976.

PUSSYCAT BY Peyo

Gag #46 appeared in *Spirou* #1593 of October 24, 1968.
It was not published in album format.

PUSSYCAT BY Peyo

Gag #47 appeared in *Spirou* #1592 of October 17, 1968.
It was later republished in album 3, page 31, in October 1977.

PUSSYCAT BY Peyo

Gag #48 appeared in *Spirou* #1591 of October 10, 1968.
It was later republished in album 1, page 43, in January 1976.

PUSSYCAT BY Peyo   THE OVEN

Gag #49 appeared in *Spirou* #1594 of October 31, 1968.
It was later republished in album 1, page 42, in January 1976.

Gag #50 appeared in *Spirou* #1507 of March 2, 1967.
It was later republished in album 2, page 38, in January 1977.

PUSSYCAT BY Peyo   TAKING A WALK

Gag #51 appeared in *Spirou* #1607 of January 30, 1969.
It was later republished in album 2, page 16, in January 1977.

PUSSYCAT BY Peyo — IN THE FISHBOWL

Gag #52 appeared in *Spirou* #1493 of November 24, 1966.
It was later republished in album 2, page 7, in January 1977.

PUSSYCAT — IGNOMINIOUSLY SENT AWAY

Gag #53 appeared in *Spirou* #1598 of November 28, 1968.
It was later republished in album 2, page 40, in January 1977.

Gag #54 appeared in *Spirou* #1505 of February 16, 1967.
It was later republished in album 2, page 10, in January 1977.

Gag #55 appeared in *Spirou* #1492 of November 17, 1966.
It was later republished in album 1, page 45, in January 1976.

PUSSYCAT

Gag # 56 appeared in *Spirou* #1600 of December 12, 1968.
It was unpublished in album format.

 PUSSYCAT BY *Peyo*   THE CUSHION

Gag #57 appeared in *Spirou* #1491 of November 10, 1966.
It was later republished in album 1, page 30, in January 1976.

 **PUSSYCAT** THE ANNOYING RIBBON

Gag #58 appeared in *Spirou* #1504 of November 9, 1967.
It was later republished in album 1, page 23, in January 1976.

PUSSYCAT HE DIDN'T LAY A PAW ON IT...

Gag #59 appeared in *Spirou* #1515 of April 27, 1967.
It was later republished in album 2, page 9, in January 1977.

PUSSYCAT BY Peyo — A HELPING CLAW

Gag #60 appeared in *Spirou* #1516 of May 4, 1967.
It was later republished in album 2, page 27, in January 1977.

PUSSYCAT BY Peyo — POLITENESS

Gag #61 appeared in *Spirou* #1517 of May 11, 1967.
It was later republished in album 3, page 21, in October 1977.

BAD WEATHER

Gag #62 appeared in album 1, page 16 in January 1976.

FLATTERING COMMENTS

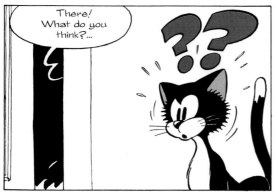

Gag #63 appeared in *Spirou* #1518 of May 18, 1967.
It was later republished in album 1, page 24, in January 1976.

PUSSYCAT

BY Peyo

Gag #64 appeared in *Spirou* #1604 of January 9, 1969.
It was not published in album format.

PUSSYCAT BY Peyo — THE POT

Gag #65 appeared in album 1, page 8, in January 1976.

49.

Gag #66 appeared in album 3, page 14, in October 1977.

PUSSYCAT BY *Peyo*   THE NATIVITY SCENE

Gag #67 appeared in album 2, page 46, in January 1977.

PUSSYCAT BY *Peyo*

Gag #68 appeared in *Spirou* #1603 of January 2, 1969.
It was later republished in album 3, page 45, in October 1977.

PUSSYCAT AN UNEXPECTED RODENT

Gag #69 appeared in *Spirou* #1519 of May 25, 1967.
It was later republished in album 3, page 11, in October 1977.

PUSSYCAT BY Peyo — THE WRECKERS

Gag #70 appeared in *Spirou* #1606 of January 23, 1969.
It was later republished in album 2, page 42, in January 1977.

PUSSYCAT BY Peyo — ANOTHER PURSUIT

Gag #71 appeared in *Spirou* #1599 of December 12, 1968.
It was later republished in album 3, page 5, in October 1977.

PUSSYCAT BY Peyo

Gag #72 appeared in *Spirou* #1520 of June 1, 1967.
It was later republished in album 3, page 26, in October 1977.

PUSSYCAT BY Peyo   THE RESTAURANT

Gag #73 appeared in *Spirou* #1556 of February 8, 1968.
It was later republished in album 3, page 35, in October 1977.

PUSSYCAT BY *Peyo*

ACTS OF WAR

Gag #74 appeared in *Spirou* #1629 of July 3, 1969.
It was later republished in album 3, page 4, in October 1977.

PUSSYCAT

THE DIFFICULT PHOTO

Gag #75 appeared in *Spirou* #1579 of July 18, 1968.
It was later republished in album 1, page 44, in January 1976.

PUSSYCAT BY Peyo

This way, you'll be warm when you go outside!

You look so ridiculous, Pussycat! Are you going to the North Pole? Ha! Ha! Ha! Ha!

Jack! Come get dressed! You have to go to your aunt's today!

Yes, Mom!

Gag #76 appeared in *Spirou* #1588 of September 19, 1968.
It was later republished in album 2, page 15, in January 1977.

PUSSYCAT BY Peyo

AN OLD PROVERB

HIC!

Heavens, is that cat drunk?!

MEOOOW—HIC!

That's normal, after all! I've always been told...

HIC!

*At night, all cats are gray!**

HIC!

Gag #77 appeared in *Spirou* #1608 of February 6, 1969.
It was later republished in album 3, page 22, in October 1977.

*Translator's note: in French "gris" can mean "gray" and "drunk."

55

 **PUSSYCAT** BY *Peyo* VIOLIN RECITAL

Gag #78 appeared in *Spirou* #1613 of March 13, 1969.
It was later republished in album 2, page 29, in January 1977.

 **PUSSYCAT** AN UNCONTROLLED SKID

Gag #79 appeared in *Spirou* #1521 of June 8, 1967 and later in #2004 of September 9, 1976.
It was later republished in album 1, page 5, in January 1976.

PUSSYCAT LET'S GATHER OUR STRENGTH

Gag #80 appeared in *Spirou* #1614 of March 20, 1969.
It was later republished in album 3, page 8, in October 1977.

PUSSYCAT BY Peyo

This gag #80 (Yes! There are two bearing the same number!) appeared in *Spirou* #1666 of March 19, 1970.
It was not published in album format.

PUSSYCAT BY Peyo

Gag #81 appeared in *Spirou* #1522 of June 15, 1967.
It was later republished in album 1, page 33, in January 1976.

PUSSYCAT   THE GIFT FOR LANGUAGES

Gag #82 appeared in *Spirou* #1619 of April 24, 1969.
It was later republished in album 1, page 31, in January 1976.

 **PUSSYCAT** SPIRIT OF IMITATION

Gag #83 appeared in *Spirou* #1558 of February 22, 1968.
It was later republished in album 1, page 27, in January 1976.

 PUSSYCAT BY *Peyo* DOUBLE STANDARDS

Gag #84 appeared in album 3, page 22, in October 1977.

PUSSYCAT BY Peyo   THE BURGLAR

Gag #85 appeared in *Spirou* #1523 of June 22, 1967.
It was later republished in album 3, page 20, in October 1977.

PUSSYCAT BY Peyo   RELENTLESS PURSUIT

Gag #86 appeared in *Spirou* #1618 of April 17, 1969.
It was later republished in album 3, page 5, in October 1977.

Gag #87 appeared in *Spirou* #1620 of May 1, 1969.
It was later republished in album 1, page 31, January 1976.

PUSSYCAT BY *Peyo* NO ENTRY

Gag #88 appeared in *Spirou* #1742 of September 2, 1971.
It was later republished in album 2, page 43, in January 1977.

Gag #89 appeared in *Spirou* #1524 of June 29, 1967.
It was later republished in album 3, page 4, in October 1977.

The adventures of PUSSYCAT by Peyo

Gag #90 appeared in *Soir Jeunesse* #90 of May 20, 1957.
It was never republished either in *Spirou* or in the comic albums. It was therefore unpublished in album format.

Gag #91 appeared in *Spirou* #1621 of May 8, 1969.
It was later republished in album 3, page 40, in October 1977.

PUSSYCAT BY Peyo   COSTUME PARTY

Gag #92 appeared in *Spirou* #1568 of May 2, 1968.
It was later republished in album 2, page 33, in January 1977.

PUSSYCAT BY Peyo

Hello?... Who took the starch I'd left in here?

Gag #93 appeared in *Spirou* #1496 of December 15, 1966.
It was later republished in album 1, page 38, in January 1976.

PUSSYCAT BY Peyo

Gag #94 appeared in *Spirou* #1534 of September 7, 1967.
It was not published in album format.

THE RETURN OF THE FISHERMAN

Gag #95 appeared in *Spirou* #1685 of July 30, 1970.
It was later republished in album 2, page 8, in January 1977.

 **PUSSYCAT** BY *Peyo*   FISH-HEAD

Gag #96 appeared in *Spirou* #1665 of March 12, 1970.
It was later republished in album 2, page 14, in January 1977.

 # PUSSYCAT SUPREME INDIFFERENCE

A. DUFAUX.
PROPS
FOR
SHOPS

Gag #97 appeared in *Spirou* #1502 of January 26, 1967.
It was later republished in album 1, page 38, in January 1976.

PUSSYCAT BY Peyo A NICE HIDEOUT

Mom! The butcher brought the meat!

Good! Put it in the cupboard before Pussycat steals it!

Pussycat!...Little Pussycat!... Okay! He's not in the kitchen!

The door's closed! The window, too!... Okay, all clear!

So there! Pussycat will have to be very clever, if he manages to steal that!

Gag #98 appeared in *Spirou* #1525 of July 6, 1967.
It was later republished in album 1, page 34, in January 1976.

PUSSYCAT BY Peyo

A CHILL

Gag #99 appeared in *Spirou* #2006 of September 23, 1976.
It was later republished in album 3, page 42, in October 1977.

PUSSYCAT

INTERRUPTED PURSUIT

Gag #100 appeared in *Spirou* #1540 of October 19, 1967 and later in #2003 of September 2, 1976.
It was next republished in album 1, page 5, in January 1976.

PUSSYCAT BY *Peyo*

Gag #101 appeared in *Spirou* #1677 of June 4, 1970.
It was later republished in album 3, page 41, in October 1977.
The artwork in the final two panels was reversed for publication here, to make the gag successful.

PUSSYCAT BY *Peyo*   A LOVELY FATE

Gag #102 appeared in *Spirou* #1526 of July 13, 1967.
It was later republished in album 1, page 46, in January 1976.

PUSSYCAT BY Peyo

Gag #103 appeared in *Spirou* #1527 of July 20, 1967.
It was later republished in album 3, page 17, in October 1977.

PUSSYCAT   EXAGGERATED CLEANLINESS

Peyo puts himself in the picture. While Walthéry or Wasterlain sometimes "poked fun" at him, it's the only time Peyo ever drew himself alongside one of his characters.

Gag #104 appeared in *Spirou* #1676 of May 28, 1970.
It was later republished in album 3, page 40, in October 1977.

PUSSYCAT BY Peyo

Gag #105 appeared in *Spirou* #1528 of July 27, 1967.
It was later republished in album 3, page 3, in October 1977.

PUSSYCAT BY Peyo STICK OUT YOUR TONGUE

Gag #106 appeared in *Spirou* #1529 August 3, 1967.
It was later republished in album 3, page 27, in October 1977.

PUSSYCAT BY *Peyo* THE TUBE OF MILK

Gag #107 appeared in black and white in *Spirou* #1632 of July 24, 1969 and in color in #1745 of September 23, 1971.
It was later republished in album 1, page 29, in January 1976.

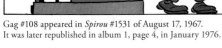 **PUSSYCAT** HOME DELIVERY

Gag #108 appeared in *Spirou* #1531 of August 17, 1967.
It was later republished in album 1, page 4, in January 1976.

PUSSYCAT — A MOMENT OF REFLECTION

Gag #109 appeared in black and white in *Spirou* #1637 of August 28, 1969 and in color in #2002 of August 26, 1976.
It was later republished in album 1, page 26, in January 1976.

PUSSYCAT BY Peyo — THE ACCIDENT

Mama! The milkman just had an accident at the corner of the street!

!

Oh?... How did it happen?

Well, it was while getting off his delivery bike! He slipped on a banana peel...

?

...And twisted his ankle!

Gag #110 appeared in *Spirou* #1532 of August 24, 1967.
It was later republished in album 1, page 4, in January 1976.

PUSSYCAT

BY Peyo

MEOOOW!

That Asian flu is just awful!

Ah! You're telling me!

?

Gag #111 appeared in *Spirou* #1662 of December 19, 1970.
It was not published in album format.

PUSSYCAT BY Peyo   A BAD REMEDY

Still nothing! That charlatan! He got me!

I'll just throw the whole worthless mixture away!

GLUG GLUG GLUG

?

I'm going to find that hairdresser and tell him what I think...

...of his much-vaunted lotion for growing hair!

Gag #112 appeared in *Spirou* #1533 of August 31, 1967.
It was later republished in album 3, page 38, in October 1977.

 **PUSSYCAT** BY *Peyo* THE REFUGE

Gag #113 appeared in *Spirou* #1656 of January 8, 1970.
It was later republished in album 3, page 16, in October 1977.

PUSSYCAT BY *Peyo* A FELINE GROWN-UP

Gag #114 appeared in *Spirou* #1634 of August 7, 1969.
It was later republished in album 2, page 33, in January 1977.

 **PUSSYCAT** BY *Peyo* TEARY-EYED

Gag #115 appeared in *Spirou* #1497 of December 22, 1966.
It was later republished in album 2, page 25, in January 1977.

 PUSSYCAT BY *Peyo* RAINY WEATHER

Gag #116 appeared in *Spirou* #1624 of May 29, 1969.
It was later republished in album 1, page 34, in January 1976.

PUSSYCAT BY Peyo

THE MUSIC-LOVER

Gag #117 appeared in album 2, page 29, in January 1977.

PUSSYCAT BY Peyo

PUSSYCAT MOUSE
3 1

A NOISE IN THE ATTIC

Gag #118 appeared in *Spirou* #1664 of March 5, 1970.
It was later republished in album 3, page 6, in October 1977.

PUSSYCAT BY Peyo — TERROR IN THE STREET

Gag #119 appeared in *Spirou* #1453 of February 17, 1966.
It was later republished in album 3, page 25, in October 1977.

PUSSYCAT — THE CHRISTMAS SPIRIT

Gag #120 appeared in album 2, page 45, in January 1977.

PUSSYCAT

BY Peyo

Gag #121 appeared in *Spirou* #1707 of December 31, 1970.
It was not published in album format.

PUSSYCAT BY Peyo

THE FRIDAY MEAL

Gag #122 appeared in *Spirou* #1443 of December 9, 1965.
It was later republished in album 2, page 6, in January 1977.

PUSSYCAT   WARMING THOSE WHO ARE COLD

Gag #123 appeared in *Spirou* #1597 of November 21, 1968.
It was later republished in album 3, page 43, in October 1977.

PUSSYCAT BY Peyo   A FRAGRANT AROMA

That's it, I'm done! It smells really good!

So much work! But that's okay...

I'm really happy with the result!

You see that you yourself can easily make a prized perfume!

Gag #124 appeared in *Spirou* #1450 of January 27, 1966.
It was later republished in album 2, page 4, in January 1977.

PUSSYCAT BY Peyo   A FINE APPEARANCE

Gag #125 appeared in *Spirou* #1557 of February 15, 1968.
It was later republished in album 2, page 35, in January 1977.

PUSSYCAT   AN AUDACIOUS DEFIANCE

Gag #126 appeared in *Spirou* #1543 of November 9, 1967.
It was later republished in album 1, page 15, in January 1976.

PUSSYCAT BY Peyo — THE RIGHT ADDRESS

Gag #127 appeared in *Spirou* #1559 of February 28, 1968.
It was later republished in album 3, page 27, in October 1977.

PUSSYCAT BY Peyo — FEAR OF WATER

Gag #128 appeared in *Spirou* #1452 of February 10, 1966.
It was later republished in album 2, page 5, in January 1977.

Gag #129 appeared in *Spirou* #1648 of November 13,1969.
It was later republished in album 3, page 28, in October 1977. The gag was rewritten here to be better understood by
an English-speaking audience. The original gag revolved around the word "Voler" which can mean "to fly" or "to steal."

 PUSSYCAT BY *Peyo* SULKING

Gag #130 appeared in *Spirou* #1645 of October 23, 1969.
It was later republished in album 3, page 15, in October 1977.

PUSSYCAT BY Peyo

Gag #131 appeared in *Spirou* #1689 of August 27, 1970.
It was later republished in album 2, page 18, in January 1977.

PUSSYCAT

BEFORE THE CORRECTION

Gag #132 appeared in *Spirou* #1448 of January 13, 1966.
It was later republished in album 3, page 28, in October 1977.

PUSSYCAT BY Peyo — A PAINFUL FALL

Gag #133 appeared in *Spirou* #1670 of April 16, 1970.
It was later republished in album 1, page 9, in January 1976.

PUSSYCAT BY Peyo

Gag #134 appeared in *Spirou* #1667 of March 26, 1970.
It was later republished in album 1, page 20, in January 1976.

Gag #135 appeared in *Spirou* #1713 of February 11, 1971.
It was later republished in album 2, page 21, in January 1977.

A "CAT" DILEMMA **PUSSYCAT** BY *Peyo*   THE PROTECTOR

Gag #136 appeared in *Spirou* #1449 of January 20, 1966.
It was later republished in album 3, page 29, in October 1977.

PUSSYCAT

DEPARTURE FOR VACATION

Gag #137 appeared in color in *Spirou* #1678 of June 11, 1970 in France and later, in black and white, in #1710 of October 21, 1971 in Belgium.
It was later republished in album 2, page 40, in January 1970.

PUSSYCAT

A QUESTION OF TASTE

Gag #138 appeared in *Spirou* #1636 of August 21, 1969.
It was later republished in album 1, page 10, in January 1976.

PUSSYCAT A VICTIM OF MECHANIZATION

Gag #139 appeared in *Spirou* #1444 of December 16, 1965.
It was later republished in albums 3, page 14, in October 1977.

PUSSYCAT CAREFULLY CHOSEN TERMS

Who's this yummy milk for? For Granny's wittle feller!

Oh! The soup is soooo good! The wittle kitty was hungry!

Oh, the sweet puddy-tat! You're puwing and wittle cuddles? And now he's going to go outside?

PURRRRRR

Be careful! Don't play with those mean doggies! They'll give you big boo-boos!

MRS. DURAND
LANGUAGE
TEACHER

Gag #140 appeared in *Spirou* #1451 of February 3, 1966.
It was later republished in album 2, page 41, in January 1977.

PUSSYCAT BY Peyo — GOOD FISHING

Gag #141 appeared in *Spirou* #1460 of April 7, 1966.
It was later republished in album 2, page 4, in January 1977.

PUSSYCAT BY Peyo — WEATHER REPORT

Gag #142 appeared in *Spirou* #1464 of May 5, 1966.
It was later republished in album 1, page 32, in January 1976.

 **PUSSYCAT** WHACKS WITH A SHOE

Gag #143 appeared in *Spirou* #1465 of May 12, 1966.
It was later republished in album 3, page 18, in October 1977.

 **PUSSYCAT** AUNT GERTRUDE'S VASE

You've spoiled us, Aunt Gertrude! That vase is splendid!

It's nothing, really! All right, it's time I go!

Ohhh! My lovely vase!

Pussycat! You klutz!

You bad cat!

Goodbye, Aunt! We're sorry! Such a beautiful vase! Pussycat will be punished severely!

Ah! Yes! He'll get what's coming to him!

Goodbye!

PUSSYCAT! COME HERE!

Good, little cat! Do you want some good milk? Did the little cat break the beautiful vase? Oh! The bad kitty!

Gag #144 appeared in *Spirou* #1462 of April 21, 1966.
It was later republished in album 2, page 37, in January 1977.

PUSSYCAT BY Peyo — A FLYING CAT

Gag #145 appeared in *Spirou* #1458 of March 24, 1966.
It was later republished in album 3, page 33, in October 1977.

PUSSYCAT BY Peyo — PRUDENT CAMOUFLAGE

Gag #146 appeared in album 2, page 32, in January 1977.

THE NEST

Gag #147 appeared in *Spirou* #1630 of July 10, 1969.
It was later republished in album 1, page 46, in January 1976.

PUSSYCAT EFFECTIVE ADVERTISEMENT

Gag #148 appeared in *Spirou* #1605 of January 16, 1969.
It was later republished in album 1, page 6, in January 1976.

PUSSYCAT BY Peyo

Gag #149 appeared in *Spirou* #1461 of April 14, 1966.
It was later republished in album 2, page 36, in January 1977.

PUSSYCAT BY Peyo — HEALTHCARE

It's no use! I give up!

There'd need to be a hundred of us! And then some!

There's no use insisting!

No! We won't be able to do it!

But he has to take that tonic! It's what the vet recommended!

Gag #150 appeared in *Spirou* #1467 of May 26, 1966.
It was later republished in album 3, page 33, in October 1977.

PUSSYCAT BY Peyo — THE CHESTNUT

Gag #151 appeared in *Spirou* #1641 of September 25, 1969.
It was later republished in album 2, page 22, in January 1977.

PUSSYCAT BY Peyo — COUNTRY COOKING

Gag #152 appeared in *Spirou* #1672 of April 30, 1970.
It was later republished in album 2, page 20, in January 1977.

Gag #153 appeared in *Spirou* #1544 of November 16, 1967.
It was later republished in album 1, page 40, in January 1976.

PUSSYCAT

BY Peyo

Gag #153 (Yes! There are two bearing the same number!) appeared in *Spirou* #1683 of July 16, 1970.
It was not published in album format.

 PUSSYCAT BY Peyo AT THE PAINTER'S

Gag #154 appeared in *Spirou* #1466 of May 19, 1966.
It was later republished in album 3, page 29, in October 1977.

PUSSYCAT BY Peyo THE FROG

Gag #155 appeared in *Spirou* #1622 of May 15, 1969.
It was later republished in album 3, page 32, in October 1977.

PUSSYCAT BY Peyo — TRACKS

Gag #156 appeared in *Spirou* #1644 of October 16, 1969.
It was later republished in album 1, page 35, in January 1976.

PUSSYCAT BY Peyo — JUDO LESSON

Gag #157 appeared in *Spirou* #1463 of April 28, 1966.
It was later republished in album 2, page 22, in January 1977.

Gag #158 appeared in *Spirou* #1454 of February 24, 1966.
It was later republished in album 2, page 25, in January 1977.

PUSSYCAT BY *Peyo* A GOOD CATCH

Gag #159 appeared in *Spirou* #1470 of June 16, 1966.
It was later republished in album 2, page 5, in January 1977.

Gag #160 appeared in *Spirou* #1626 of June 12, 1969.
It was later republished in album 2, page 23, in January 1977.

Pussycat! Come see the beautiful fish they just brought in!

Gag #161 appeared in *Spirou* #1535 of September 14, 1967.
It was later republished in album 2, page 9, in January 1977.

PUSSYCAT BY Peyo   THE CAGE

Gag #162 appeared in *Spirou* #1471 of June 23, 1966.
It was later republished in album 2, page 13, in January 1977.

PUSSYCAT BY Peyo   THE LEOPARD

Gag #163 appeared in *Spirou* #1472 of June 30, 1966.
It was later republished in album 3, page 25, in October 1977.

Gag #164 appeared in *Spirou* #1483 of September 15, 1966.
It was later republished in album 1, page 8, in January 1976.

PUSSYCAT

RAID ON THE AQUARIUM

Gag #165 appeared in *Spirou* #1478 of August 11, 1966.
It was later republished in album 2, page 13, in January 1977.

PUSSYCAT BY *Peyo* — A LONG BAKE

Gag #166 appeared in *Spirou* #1473 of July 7, 1966.
It was later republished in album 2, page 41, in January 1977.

PUSSYCAT by Peyo and DE GIETER

Gag #167 appeared in *Spirou* #1653 of December 18, 1969.
It was not published in album format.

PUSSYCAT

by Peyo

Honestly, have you see this chaton?!* What happened to it?

?

It's all twisted up!

I'll try to straighten it with some pincers.

!?

But tomorrow, take this ring to the jewelers!

*Translator's note: A "chaton," in French, can mean either a bezel or a kitten.
Gag #168 appeared in *Spirou* #1474 of July 14, 1966.
It was not published in album format.

PUSSYCAT
BY Peyo   NOISY GIFTS

What did you ask Santa Claus for?

Tons of things!

Some beautiful picture books, candy, and chocolate!

I asked for a construction set!

And also for a doll that goes: ≥WAAAAH! WAAAAH!≤ and a piano!

And a drum, a trumpet, a slingshot, a cap gun! BANG! BANG!

!?

HISSSSSS
HISSSS

?

Gag #169 appeared in *Spirou* #1652 of December 11, 1969.
It was later republished in album 2, page 45, in January 1977.

 **PUSSYCAT**

Gag#170 appeared in *Spirou* #1446 of December 30, 1965.
It was later republished in album 3, page 46, in October 1977.

PUSSYCAT BY Peyo

Gag #171 appeared in *Spirou* #1625 of June 5, 1969.
It was later republished in album 2, page 24, in January 1977.

 **PUSSYCAT** BY Peyo ANIMAL PROTECTION

Gag #172 appeared in *Spirou* #1482 of September 8, 1966.
It was later republished in album 1, page 32, in January 1976.

PUSSYCAT BY Peyo REMINDER

Gosh! I mustn't forget to call Yves this afternoon! I'll make a knot in my handkerchief!

Yes! But if I don't have to blow my nose, I'll forget! That's not a solution!

It'd have to be something in plain view the whole time! Hmm...

Gag #173 appeared in *Spirou* #1690 of September 3, 1970.
It was later republished in album 2, page 18, in January 1977.

Gag #174 appeared in *Spirou* #1442 of December 2, 1965.
It was later republished in album 3, page 19, in October 1977.

Gag #175 appeared in *Spirou* #1642 of October 2, 1969.
It was later republished in album 3, page 15, in October 1977.

PUSSYCAT BY Peyo

Gag #176 appeared in *Spirou* #1475 of July 21, 1966.
It was later republished in album 1, page 13, in January 1976.

PUSSYCAT BY Peyo   DOORBELL NUMBER

Gag #177 appeared in *Spirou* #1684 of July 23, 1970.
It was later republished in album 3, page 36, in October 1977.

PUSSYCAT BY Peyo   HUNTING OUTFIT

Gag #178 appeared in *Spirou* #1476 of July 28, 1966.
It was later republished in album 2, page 31, in January of 1977.

PUSSYCAT BY Peyo   THE DREAM

Gag #179 appeared in *Spirou* #1485 of September 29, 1966.
It was later republished in album 1, page 39, in January 1976.

PUSSYCAT BY *Peyo* THE CAT SHOW

Gag #180 appeared in *Spirou* #1997 of July 22, 1966.
It was later republished in album 1, page 19, in January 1976.

 PUSSYCAT BY *Peyo* A BELL RINGS, RINGS...

Gag #181 appeared in *Spirou* #1459 of March 31, 1966.
It was later republished in album 1, page 21, in January 1976.

 **PUSSYCAT** A GASTRONOMICAL PACKAGE

Gag #182 appeared in *Spirou* #1511 of March 30, 1967.
It was later republished in album 1, page 37, in January 1976.

 PUSSYCAT BY *Peyo* A FEAR OF WATER

Gag #183 appeared in *Spirou* #1675 of May 21, 1970.
It was later republished in album 3, page 38, in October 1977.

Gag #184 appeared in *Spirou* #1671 of April 23, 1970.
It was later republished in album 2, page 21, in January 1977.

PUSSYCAT BY *Peyo* CUCKOO!

Gag #185 appeared in *Spirou* #1480 of August 25, 1966.
It was later republished in album 1, page 44, in January 1976.

Gag #186 appeared in *Spirou* #1457 of March 17, 1966.
It was later republished in album 2, page 23, in January 1977.

 **PUSSYCAT**

APPETIZING MOOING

Gag #187 appeared in *Spirou* #1560 of March 7, 1968.
It was later republished in album 1, page 11, in January 1976.

PUSSYCAT BY Peyo

Gag #188 appeared in *Spirou* #1640 of September 18, 1969.
It was later republished in album 1, page 24, in January 1976.

PUSSYCAT BY Peyo

Gag #189 appeared in *Spirou* #1681 of July 2, 1970.
It was later republished in album 1, page 22, in January 1976.

PUSSYCAT BY *Peyo*

MADE IN JAPAN

Gag #190 appeared in album 1, page 12, in October 1977

PUSSYCAT

FISHING TALE

Gag #191 appeared in *Spirou* #1477 of August 4, 1966.
It was later republished in album 2, page 12, in January 1977.

PUSSYCAT BY *Peyo* THE TONIC

Gag #192 appeared in *Spirou* #1439 of November 11, 1965.
It was later republished in album 1, page 15, in January 1976.

PUSSYCAT BY *Peyo* AT THE BEACH

Gag #193 appeared in *Spirou* #1469 of June 9, 1966.
It was later republished in album 2, page 12, in January 1977.

LABELING ERROR

Gag #194 appeared in *Spirou* #1658 of January 22, 1970.
It was later republished in album 1, page 10, in January 1976.

PUSSYCAT BY *Peyo*

Gag #195 appeared in *Spirou* #1693 of September 24, 1970.
It was later republished in album 2, page 30, in January 1977.

FISHING PROHIBITED

Gag #196 appeared in *Spirou* #1545 of November 23, 1967.
It was later republished in album 1, page 27, in January 1976.

 PUSSYCAT BY *Peyo*   THE HOTEL MOUSE

Gag #197 appeared in Spirou #1643 of October 9, 1969.
It was later republished in album 3, page 10, in October 1977.

PUSSYCAT BY Peyo — THE PACKAGE

Gag #198 appeared in *Spirou* #1682 of July 9, 1970.
It was later republished in album 3, page 12, in October 1977.

PUSSYCAT BY Peyo — LIGHTER THAN AIR

Gag #199 appeared in *Spirou* #1441 of November 25, 1965.
It was later republished in album 1, page 29, in January 1976.

Gag #200 appeared in *Spirou* #1639 of September 11, 1969.
It was later republished in album 1, page 33, in January 1976.

PUSSYCAT BY Peyo

CLEANLINESS

Gag #201 appeared in album 2, page 17, in January 1977.

THE NIGHT BEFORE GOING BACK-TO-SCHOOL

Gag #202 appeared in *Spirou* #1481 of September 1, 1966.
It was later republished in album 2, page 19, in January 1977.

PUSSYCAT BY Peyo   TIT FOR TAT

Gag #203 appeared in *Spirou* #1440 of November 18, 1965.
It was later republished in album 3, page 13, in October 1977.

PUSSYCAT

LANGUAGE CLASSES

Gag #204 appeared in *Spirou* #1479 of August 18, 1966.
It was later republished in album 1, page 19, in January 1976.

PUSSYCAT

ORDERS ARE ORDERS

Gag #205 appeared in *Spirou* #1537 of September 28, 1967.
It was later republished in album 2, page 42, in January 1977.

PUSSYCAT BY Peyo — WATER SQUIRTS

Gag #206 appeared in *Spirou* #1998 of July 29, 1976.
It was later republished in album 1, page 30, in January 1976.

PUSSYCAT AN APPETIZING SMELL

Gag #207 appeared in *Spirou* #2001 of August 19, 1976.
It was later republished in album 1, page 39, in January 1976.

PUSSYCAT BY Peyo

Gag #208 appeared in *Spirou* #1539 of October 12, 1967.
It was later republished in album 2, page 39, in January 1977.

PUSSYCAT BY Peyo   LOUDER, PLEASE!

Gag #209 appeared in *Spirou* #1996 of July 15, 1976.
It was next republished in album 3, page 19, in October 1977. A slightly different version of this gag,
signed by De Gieter, appeared in *Spirou* #1715, numbered 249 (see page 142 of this collected edition).

PUSSYCAT BY Peyo FRIGHTENING SPECTACLE

Gag #210 appeared in album 3, page 35, in October 1977.

PUSSYCAT BY Peyo MEANS OF DEFENSE

Gag #211 appeared in *Spirou* #1995 of July 8, 1976.
It was later republished in album 3, page 13, in October 1977.

Gag #212 appeared in *Spirou* #1456 of March 10, 1966.
It was later republished in album 1, page 45, in January 1976.

 PUSSYCAT BY *Peyo* THE BIG STAR

Gag #213 appeared in *Spirou* #1999 of August 5, 1976.
It was later republished in album 1, page 23, in January 1976.

PUSSYCAT BY Peyo

INNOCENT GAMES

Gag #214 appeared in *Spirou* #1488 of October 20, 1966.
It was later republished in album 2, page 20, in January 1977.

PUSSYCAT BY Peyo

A NICE STORY

Gag #215 appeared in *Spirou* #1530 of August 10, 1967.
It was later republished in album 1, page 14, in January 1976.

Gag #216 appeared in *Spirou* #1489 of October 27, 1966.
It was later republished in album 3, page 34, in October 1977.

PUSSYCAT AND A HAPPY NEW YEAR

Gag #217 appeared in *Spirou* #1706 of December 24, 1970.
It was later republished in album 2, page 46, in January 1977. A slightly different version of this gag, signed by De Gieter, appeared in black and white in
Spirou #1706, numbered 255 (see page 145 of this complete collection).

PUSSYCAT BY Peyo — END-OF-YEAR WORRIES

Happy New Year, Cousin Hortense, and good health to you! Johnny, kiss your cousin!... Would you like a small glass of port?... My the children have grown!... You've not changed a bit, cousin! Ah!... If it weren't for my rheumatism! The doctor told me that...

We should see each other more often! We have to go! Johnny, kiss your cousin!... Hello, Uncle Jules! Happy New Year and good health to you! Our best wishes!... You'll have a small glass of port! Johnny! Did you kiss Uncle Jules?

We still have to go to Aunt Lulu's and Cousin Albert's! Johnny! Kiss your uncle!... Happy New Year, Lulu! Johnny! Kiss your aunt!... Port?... Happy, Happy New Year! Johnny! Kiss your cousin!... Will you have a...

And that's for tomorrow!

THURSDAY 31 DECEMBER

Gag #218 appeared in album 3, page 46, in October 1977.

PUSSYCAT BY Peyo — MISCALCULATION

Gag #219 appeared in *Spirou* #1487 of October 13, 1966.
It was later republished in album 1, page 26, in January 1976.

Gag #220 appeared in *Spirou* #1445 of December 23, 1965.
It was later republished in album 3, page 43, in October 1977.

PUSSYCAT BY Peyo

Gag #221 appeared in *Spirou* #1447 of January 6, 1966.
It was later republished in album 1, page 3, in January 1976.

PUSSYCAT BY Peyo — NATURAL SCIENCES

Gag #222 appeared in *Spirou* #1438 of November 4, 1965. It was the very first Pussycat gag to appear in Spirou.
It was later republished in album 2, page 43, in January 1977.

PUSSYCAT BY Peyo — DISAPPOINTED HOPE

*Translator's note: Pussycat doesn't realize that the ballet students at the Paris Opera are called "petits rats."
Gag #223 appeared in *Spirou* #1484 of September 22, 1966.
It was later republished in album 3, page 10, in October 1977.

 LOST AND FOUND

PUSSYCAT

THE DISAPPEARANCE

Gag #224 appeared in *Spirou* #1455 of March 3, 1966.
It was later republished in album 2, page 19, in January 1977.

PUSSYCAT BY Peyo

TOO KIND

Gag #225 appeared in *Spirou* #1649 of November 20, 1969.
It was later republished in album 2, page 37, in January 1977.

PUSSYCAT BY Peyo

We can't go on like this! We absolutely must reduce our living expenses!

We could, for example, do without chicken on Sundays! And have fish less often! It's overpriced!

On the other hand, we can eat pasta more often! And less meat! Vegetarians don't eat any and...

!

Gag #226 appeared in *Spirou* #1486 of October 6, 1966.
It was later republished in album 1, page 36, in January 1976.

PUSSYCAT BY Peyo   CARNAVAL CAT

Daddy! Did you see Pussycat?

Hmm?

AAAH!

It's-- It's horrible! What happened to him?!...

Well it's Carnaval! So I disguised him as the cat o' nine-tails!

!

Gag #227 appeared in album 2, page 32, in January 1977. A different version of this gag, signed by De Gieter, appeared in *Spirou* #1766, numbered 258 (see page 147 of this edition).

PUSSYCAT BY Peyo — THE BALLOON

Gag #228 appeared in album 2, page 17, in January 1977.

PUSSYCAT BY Peyo — THE TONIC

Gag #229 appeared in *Spirou* #1669 in April 9, 1970.
It was later republished in album 3, page 36, in October 1977.

Gag #230 appeared in *Spirou* #1668 of April 2, 1970.
It was later republished in album 2, page 14, in January 1977.

PUSSYCAT BY *Peyo*   APRIL FOOL*

Pussycat! Do you want some whipping cream?

If you don't come, I'll give it to the neighbor's cat!

*Translator's note: As indicated earlier, French-speakers say "April fish" for April Fool.
Gag #231 appeared in *Spirou* #1490 of November 3, 1966.
It was later republished in album 3, page 34, in October 1977.

Gag #232 appeared in *Spirou* #1468 of June 2, 1966.
It was later republished in album 2, page 11, in January 1977.

PUSSYCAT

by **Peyo** and *De Gieter*

Gag #233 appeared in *Spirou* #1609 of February 2, 1969.
It was not published in album format.

PUSSYCAT

Gag #234 appeared in *Spirou* #1612 of March 6, 1969.
It was not published in album format.

PUSSYCAT

Gag #235 appeared in *Spirou* #1638 of September 4, 1969.
It was not published in album format.

PUSSYCAT

by **Peyo** and *De Gieter*

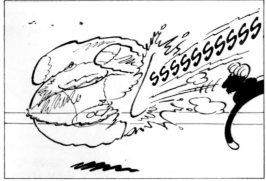

Gag #236 appeared in *Spirou* #1611 of February 27, 1969.
It was not published in album format.

PUSSYCAT by Peyo — A COLD FRY

Gag #237 appeared in *Spirou* #1610 of February 20, 1969.
It was later republished in album 2, page 8, in January 1977.

PUSSYCAT BY Peyo

Come on, Grandpa. You have to drink the whole cup of milk. That's what the doctor recommended!

‡BLAH!‡

Hey, Pussycat! Here's some good milk for you!

!

You see, that wasn't so bad and also, to make you happy, I added in a few drops of your favorite liquor!

‡Hic!‡

238

Gag #238 appeared in *Spirou* #1711 of January 28, 1971.
It was later republished in album 1, page 12, in January 1976.

PUSSYCAT

by **Peyo** and *De Gieter*

What yucky weather!

I wouldn't put a dog out in that!

Or a cat either, right, Pussycat?

?

MEOOOooooOoWW

?

‡!

238

Gag #239 appeared in *Spirou* #1619 of April 24, 1969.
It was not published in album format.

PUSSYCAT BY Peyo — ILL-TEMPERED

Gag #240 appeared in *Spirou* #1708 of January 7, 1971.
It was later republished in album 1, page 14, in January 1976.

PUSSYCAT BY Peyo

Gag # 241 appeared in the "*dossier détente*" supplement of *Spirou* #1694 of October 1, 1970.
It was not published in album format.

PUSSYCAT

by **Peyo** and *De Gieter*

Gag #242 appeared in *Spirou* #1709 of January 14, 1971.
It was not published in album format.

 **PUSSYCAT** BY *Peyo*   PROTECTION

Gag #243 appeared in *Spirou* #1696 of October 15, 1970.
It was later republished in album 3, page 7, in October 1977.

The teacher taught me a new piece today!

?

Beautiful, isn't it?

EEEEEEK EEEEK

Oh, darn! I'll need new catgut to continue!

TSOING

Gag #244 appeared in *Spirou* #1717 of March 11, 1971.
It was later republished in album 2, page 27, in January 1977.

PUSSYCAT BY Peyo

It's nothing serious, ma'am, just a slight food poisoning. A treatment of dairy products and, in a few days, he'll be cured!

?

Thanks, Doctor!

MILK MILK MILK

Meooow!

Heavens! Pussycat, too! I'll have to call the vet!

I'm the veterinarian. For food poisoning, a shot will do. Where is he?

Gag #245 appeared in *Spirou* #1705 of December 17, 1970.
It was not published in album format.

PUSSYCAT BY Peyo

Gag #246 appeared in *Spirou* #1695 of October 8, 1970.
It was later republished in album 3, page 7, in October 1977.

PUSSYCAT BY Peyo

Gag #247 appeared in *Spirou* #1719 of March 25, 1971.
It was not published in album format.

PUSSYCAT
BY Peyo

Gag #248 appeared in *Spirou* #1718 of March 18, 1971.
It was not published in album format.

PUSSYCAT
BY Peyo

Gag #249 appeared in *Spirou* #1715 of February 25, 1971.
A slightly different version of this gag appeared in *Spirou* #1996, numbered 209, and was republished in album 3 (see page 122 of the present complete collection).

PUSSYCAT BY Peyo

Gag #250 appeared in *Spirou* #1704 of December 10, 1970.
It was not published in album format.

PUSSYCAT BY Peyo

Gag #251 appeared in *Spirou* #1722 of April 15, 1971.
It was not published in album format.

PUSSYCAT

Gag #252 appeared in *Spirou* #1703 of December 3, 1970.
It was later republished in album 3, page 16, in October 1977.

Despite our best efforts, we failed to locate gag #253. Either Peyo "skipped" a number, and this gag doesn't exist, or, as some think, it's the editorial content "The Dignified Turkey," which appeared in the *Journal de Spirou* #1706 of December 24, 1970 (thus, after gag #252 and before gag #254), and which serves as #253. Or this gag does exist. And we'd be very happy to add it in lieu of this text in future editions of this complete collection. If you have any information on this subject, please don't hesitate to bring it to our attention. Contact us at Salicrup@papercutz.com or write to us at Jim Salicrup, Papercutz, 160 Broadway, Suite 700, East Wing, New York, NY 10038.

PUSSYCAT BY *Peyo*

Gag #254 appeared in *Spirou* #1712 of February 4, 1971.
It was not published in album format.

PUSSYCAT BY **Peyo** and *De Gieter*

Gag #255 appeared in *Spirou* #1706 of December 24, 1970. A slightly different version of this gag, in color, appeared in Spirou #1706, numbered 217, and was republished in album 2 (see page 126 of the present complete collection).

PUSSYCAT BY Peyo — THE CHICK

Gag #256 appeared in *Spirou* #1721 of April 8, 1971.
It was later republished in album 1, page 21, in January 1976.

PUSSYCAT BY Peyo — THE SEDUCTION

Gag #257 appeared in *Spirou* #1720 of April 1, 1971.
It was later republished in album 2, page 35, in January 1977.

PUSSYCAT

by **Peyo** **and** *De Gieter*

Gag #258 appeared in *Spirou* #1766 of February 17, 1972.
A different version of this gag appeared in album 2, page 32, numbered 227 (see page 131 of this complete edition).

PUSSYCAT

BY Peyo

Gag #259 appeared in the "*dossier détente*" supplement of *Spirou* #1733 of July 1, 1971.
It was not published in album format.

PUSSYCAT BY *Peyo*

Gag #260 appeared in *Spirou* #1740 of August 19, 1971.
It was later republished in album 1, page 16, in January 1976.

PUSSYCAT BY *Peyo*

Gag #261 appeared in *Spirou* #1758 of December 23, 1971.
It was later republished in album 1, page 12, in January 1976.

PUSSYCAT

THE VACUUM CLEANER

Gag #270 appeared in *Spirou* #1791 of August 10, 1972.
It was later republished in album 3, page 6, in October 1977.

PUSSYCAT BY *Peyo*

THE DEEP SEA DIVER

Gag #271 appeared in *Spirou* #1796 of September 14, 1972.
It was later republished in album 2, page 6, in January 1977.

PUSSYCAT
by Peyo

 and *DE GIETER*

Gag #272 appeared in the supplement to *Spirou* #1803 of November 2, 1972.
It was not published in album format.

PUSSYCAT
by Peyo

 and *DE GIETER*

Gag #273 appeared in *Spirou* #1800 of October 12, 1972.
It was not published in album format.

PUSSYCAT

by Peyo

and *DE GIETER*

Gag #1 appeared in *Spirou* #1827 of April 19, 1973.
It was not published in album format. This gag took up a full page

155.

Gag #2 appeared in *Spirou* #1804 of November 9, 1972.
It was later republished in album 3, page 23, in October 1977. This gag took up a full page.

PUSSYCAT
by Peyo

 and *DE GIETER*

Gag #3 appeared in *Spirou* #1855 of November 1, 1973.
It was not published in album format. This gag took up a full page.

157.

·PUSSYCAT· PEYO··

Gag #1D appeared in *Spirou* #2007 of September 30, 1976.
It was not published in album format.

·PUSSYCAT· ·PEYO·

Gag #2D appeared in *Spirou* #2009 of October 14, 1976.
It was not published in album format.

Gag #3D appeared in *Spirou* #2008 of October 7, 1976.
It was not published in album format.

·PUSSYCAT ···················· ············· PEYO ··

Gag #4D appeared in *Spirou* #2010 of October 21, 1976.
It was not published in album format.

Gag #5D appeared in *Spirou* #2012 of November 4, 1976.
It was not published in album format.

·PUSSYCAT· · PEYO ·

Gag #6D appeared in *Spirou* #2019 of December 23, 1976.
It was not published in album format.

PUSSYCAT........... ......PEYO..

Sure, he dives great, but the trouble is that he hates water!

Gag #7D appeared in *Spirou* #2021 of January 6, 1977.
It was unpublished in album format.

★ ★ ★ *Pussycat* by **Peyo**  ★ ★ ★ ★ *and DE GIETER* ★ ★ ★

I'm going shopping for dinner. Meanwhile, Pussycat, you better be very good!

--We've learned that a tanker truck has flipped over into the river--

--Warning! The fish are unsafe for consumption!

That's nice! Pussycat was very good!

Gag #8D appeared in *Spirou* #2026 of February 10, 1977.
It was unpublished in album format.

Gag #9D appeared in *Spirou* #2033 of March 31, 1977.
It was unpublished in album format.

Are you coming, Pussycat? We're going to collect starfish!

Careful! The rocks are slippery!

Hey! I found some! And you, Pussycat?

Pussycat, where are you?

Gag #10D appeared in *Spirou* #2036 of April 21, 1977.
It was not published in album format.

Gag #11D appeared in *Spirou* #2038 of May 5, 1977.
It was not published in album format.

Gag #12D appeared in *Spirou* #2042 of June 2, 1977.
It was not published in album format.

Gag #13D appeared in *Spirou* #2044 of June 16, 1977.
It was not published in album format.

Gag #14D appeared in *Spirou* #2045 of June 23, 1977.
It was not published in album format.

Gag #15D appeared in *Spirou* #2046 of June 30, 1977.
It was not published in album format.

Pussycat by Peyo
and DE GIETER

Gag #16D appeared in *Spirou* #2047 of July 7, 1977.
It was not published in album format.

PUSSYCAT BY Peyo

Gag #274 appeared in *Schtroumpf* magazine #13 of October 1990.
It was not published in album format. Author: Eric Closter.

PUSSYCAT BY Peyo

Gag #275 appeared in *Schtroumpf* magazine #14 of November 1990.
It was not published in album format. Author: Éric Closter.

PUSSYCAT BY Peyo

Gag #276 appeared in *Schtroumpf* magazine #15 of December 1990.
It was not published in album format. Author: Éric Closter.

PUSSYCAT BY Peyo

Gag #277 appeared in *Schtroumpf* magazine #16 of January 1991.
It was not published in album format. Author: Daniel Desorgher.

PUSSYCAT BY Peyo

Gag #278 appeared in *Schtroumpf* magazine #17 of February 1991.
It was not published in album format. Author: Daniel Desorgher.

PUSSYCAT BY Peyo

Gag #279 appeared in *Schtroumpf* magazine #18 of March 1991.
It was not published in album format. Author: Daniel Desorgher.

PUSSYCAT BY Peyo

Gag #280 appeared in *Schtroumpf* magazine #19 of April 1991.
It was not published in album format. Author: Daniel Desorgher.

PUSSYCAT BY Peyo

Gag #281 appeared in *Schtroumpf* magazine of May 20, 1991.
It was not published in album format. Author: Philippe Delzenne.

PUSSYCAT BY Peyo

Gag #282 appeared in *Schtroumpf* magazine #21 of June 1991.
It was not published in album format. Author: Philippe Delzenne.

PUSSYCAT BY Peyo

Gag #283 appeared in *Schtroumpf* magazine #22 of July 1991.
It was not published in album format. Author: Philippe Delzenne.

PUSSYCAT BY Peyo

Gag #284 appeared in *Schtroumpf* magazine #23 of August 1991.
It was not published in album format. Author: Philippe Delzenne.

PUSSYCAT BY Peyo

Gag #285 appeared in *Schtroumpf* magazine #24 of September 1991.
It was not published in album format. Author: Daniel Desorgher.

PUSSYCAT BY Peyo

Gag #286 appeared in *Schtroumpf* magazine #25 of October 1991.
It was not published in album format. Author: Philippe Delzenne.

PUSSYCAT BY Peyo

Gag #287 appeared in *Schtroumpf* magazine #26 of November 1991.
It was not published in album format. Author: Philippe Delzenne.

PUSSYCAT BY Peyo

Gag #288 appeared in *Schtroumpf* magazine #27 of December 1991.
It was not published in album format. Author: Philippe Delzenne.

PUSSYCAT BY Peyo

Gag #289 appeared in *Schtroumpf* magazine #28 of January 1992.
It was not published in album format. Author: Philippe Delzenne.

PUSSYCAT BY *Peyo*

Gag #290 appeared in *Schtroumpf* magazine #30 of March 1992.
It was not published in album format. Author: Philippe Delzenne.

PUSSYCAT BY *Peyo*

Gag #291 appeared in *Schtroumpf* magazine #31 of April 1992.
It was not published in album format. Author: Philippe Delzenne.

PUSSYCAT BY *Peyo*

Gag #292 appeared in *Schtroumpf* magazine #32 of May 1992.
It was not published in album format. Author: Philippe Delzenne.

PUSSYCAT BY *Peyo*

Gag #293 appeared in *Schtroumpf* magazine #33 of June 1992.
It was not published in album format.

PUSSYCAT BY Peyo

Gag #294 appeared in *Schtroumpf* magazine #34 of July 1992.
It was not published in album format. Author: Philippe Delzenne.

As noted previously, Peyo had selected the gags that would comprise the three PUSSYCAT comic albums and had grouped them thematically without taking their chronology into account. Each chapter heading consisted of a short introductory text and a drawing. They are all brought together here in the following pages, accompanied by the illustrations from the title pages.

THAT'S PUSSYCAT

Peyo

DUPUIS

Title page illustration from album 1, *Ça, c'est Poussy,* which appeared in January 1976.

PUSSYCAT

isn't so very different
from all the other cats
you know. In a single day,
he lives more than
a thousand adventures:
you'd need a whole
volume to read all of
them. But you're
holding that volume
in your hand.

Page 3 of album 1, *Ça, c'est Poussy,* which appeared in January 1976.

PUSSYCAT

is always very nice
with those he meets,
even if the neighborhood
dogs like to pester him
sometimes. But be
reassured, they're all
bark and no bite.

Page 13 of album 1, *Ça, c'est Poussy,* which appeared in January 1976.

PUSSYCAT

is always ready
to celebrate spring.
But what he likes
the most is Easter;
it's then when
he looks a little
silly.

Page 20 of album 1, *Ça, c'est Poussy*, which appeared in January 1976.

PUSSYCAT

is a little cat who's
very cute and, above
all, very stylish. Look
how proud he is when
someone notices
his nice outfit!

Page 22 of album 1, *Ça, c'est Poussy*, which appeared in January 1976.

PUSSYCAT

is always ready
to make new friends.
He's interested in other
animals because he's
a pretty smart cat.

Page 25 of album 1, *Ça, c'est Poussy*, which appeared in January 1976.

PUSSYCAT

is a very clever kitten,
who always has a good
trick up his sleeve.
That's why he always
gets out of a tight spot
with distinction.

Page 28 of album 1, *Ça, c'est Poussy*, which appeared in January 1976.

PUSSYCAT

may be something of a gourmand. In any case, that's what they claim. But it's not his fault if so many good things pass by right under his nose.

Page 36 of album 1, *Ça, c'est Poussy,* which appeared in January 1976.

PUSSYCAT

is birds' best friend. So much so, he can't do without them and wants only to get very, very close to them.

Page 43 of album 1, *Ça, c'est Poussy,* which appeared in January 1976.

DON'T DO THAT, PUSSYCAT

Illustration from the title page of album #2, *Faut pas Poussy*, which appeared in January 1977.

PUSSYCAT

is a very nice cat,
but with one fault: he'd
do anything for a little
bit of fish. Don't be
annoyed with him:
how many anglers
are there who
do likewise?

Page 3 of album 2, *Faut pas Poussy,* which appeared in January 1977.

PUSSYCAT

and children get
along well together,
for they have mischief
and a good mood
in common.

Page 15 of album 2, *Faut pas Poussy,* which appeared in January 1977.

PUSSYCAT

is a little cat chock
full of kindness, and
all of his deeds
come straight from
his kind heart.

Page 24 of album 2, *Faut pas Poussy,* which appeared in January 1977.

PUSSYCAT

has two pretty ears,
but doesn't like for
them to be deafened
by music. Which proves
that music doesn't
always charm
the savage beast.

Page 26 of album 2, *Faut pas Poussy,* which appeared in January 1977.

PUSSYCAT

is the cutest of all little cats, and have you noticed how practically nothing dressed him up?

Page 30 of album 2, *Faut pas Poussy*, which appeared in January 1977.

PUSSYCAT

is tenderhearted and sometimes lets himself get carried away with affection. All it takes are two pretty eyes to turn his head Men and cats are often very much alike!

Page 34 of album 2, *Faut pas Poussy*, which appeared in January 1977.

PUSSYCAT

is sometimes
responsible for small
blunders. But after all,
it's because he's
always hard at work.
Those who
never do anything
never make any
mistakes.

Page 36 of album 2, *Faut pas Poussy,* which appeared in January 1977.

PUSSYCAT

is like all cats, he can feel
at ease with several masters.
He loves people who give him
something to eat, and
if he does obey, it's only
when it suits him.

Page 39 of album 2, *Faut pas Poussy,* which appeared in January 1977.

PUSSYCAT

likes Christmas
because of the gifts
and the white snow.
But for him, the most
important thing is
the turkey!

Page 44 of album 2, *Faut pas Poussy,* which appeared in January 1977.

PUSSYCAT PUSHED

by *Peyo*

Title page illustration from album 3, *Poussy Poussa*, which appeared in October 1977.

PUSSYCAT

goodheartedly does his
job as a cat and chases
mice every time he sees
them. But since he is nice,
he sometimes doesn't
end up munching on
his friends, the mice…

Page 3 of album 3, *Poussy Poussa,* which appeared in October 1977.

PUSSYCAT

likes the night, and
during his walks, under
the moonbeams,
he sings out his most
melodious songs.

Page 17 of album 3, *Poussy Poussa,* which appeared in October 1977.

PUSSYCAT

is capable of anything,
of the best and the worst.
You never know what
trick he'll play in
the following minutes.
All that you know is
that it'll be something
unexpected.

Page 24 of album 3, *Poussy Poussa*, which appeared in October 1977.

PUSSYCAT

has one fault: he's a thieving cat.
His appetite is too much
for him to hear the voice
of his conscience:
you can't reason
with a starving cat.

Page 26 of album 3, *Poussy Poussa*, which appeared in October 1977.

PUSSYCAT

is capable of anything,
of the best and the worst.
You never know what
trick he'll play in
the following minutes.
All that you know is
that it'll be something
unexpected.

Page 31 of album 3, *Poussy Poussa*, which appeared in October 1977.

PUSSYCAT

is so pretty that you
wonder why his masters
so often try to pretty
him up even more.
In any case, he already
finds himself beautiful
enough as is.

Page 37 of album 3, *Poussy Poussa*, which appeared in October 1977.

PUSSYCAT

knows well how to take advantage of every season. In the depths of summer or in the heart of winter, he's always ready for tons of adventures or misadventures.

Page 41 of album 3, *Poussy Poussa,* which appeared in October 1977.

PUSSYCAT

At the beginning of the year, when you receive kind wishes, you'd rather it be done in an original fashion. Especially if the wishes are presented by PUSSYCAT.

Page 45 of album 3, *Poussy Poussa,* which appeared in October 1977.